Copyright @ 2016

REGIONAL MANAGEMENT SERVICES INC.
P. O. BOX 845
CHEAPSIDE
BRIDGETOWN
BARBADOS
BB 11000

Email: rmsinc@caribsurf.com

All rights reserved.
No part of this publication may be produced or transmitted in any form or by any means, electronic or mechanical, including photocopying, recording, or any information storage and retrieval system, without the permission of the author.

de Peiza, Dennis: INTRODUCTION TO THE WORLD OF WORK

ISBN 978-976-8253-05-7

This publication is dedicated to the orientation of entrants into the world of work. It is also excellent reading for employees who are or have been employed, and are engaged in a training and retraining programmes that address the rights, roles, responsibilities, expectations of workers, labour practices and workplace standards.

This publication is best suited for use in education and training institutions, primarily Secondary and High Schools, Colleges, Universities, Labour Colleges and other training institutions.

TABLE OF CONTENTS

CHAPTER 1:
UNIONIZATION: LABOUR LAWS, PRACTICES AND WORKPLACE STANDARDS

The Significance of Industrial Relations	1
The Existence of Trade Unions	2
Trade Union Recognition	3
The Right to be Unionized	5
Workers' Rights	6
Occupational Safety and Health: Responsibilities of the Employer and Employee	8

CHAPTER 2:
TOOL KIT FOR THE WORLD OF WORK

Job Recruitment	10
A Job vs. A Career	12
Starting a New Job	13
Interviewing Techniques	15
The Contract of Employment	16
Workplace Etiquette	19
Dressing Appropriately for Work	20

CHAPTER 3:
WORKPLACE REQUIREMENTS AND EXPECTATIONS

Team Building	22
Applying Universal Ethical Principles in the Workplace	25
Dress: Deportment and the Corporate Image	26
Enhancing Workplace Productivity	27
Freedom of Speech	28
Service Excellence	30

CHAPTER 4:
EMPLOYEE CONCERNS

Guide to Retaining Employment	32
Power vs. Authority	33
The Dictates of Leadership	35
Lay Off and Retrenchment of Workers	36
The Principle of Last In and First Out	38

PREFACE

In the world of the 21st Century, much attention is being paid to the subject of human resource development. The objective of this thrust is the development of an educated, knowledgeable, skilled, productive and efficient workforce. For this to be achieved, it requires a commitment to the training and retraining of the workforce.

This work is a dedicated source of information, which is directed at orienting new entrants into the work of work, whether they are full time, temporary, part-time, casual or contract workers. It is important that those entering the world of work, who primarily do so without any work experience, are not however ignorant of what the world of work expects of them.

It is for this reason, that this text provides insights into best practices, processes and procedures that are to be followed in the world of work. Those who are exposed to this text will find relevant Industrial Relations information, which would serve to guide their workplace behaviour and actions.

The text is dedicated to promoting accepted workplace standards and best practices. It offers readers insights of the do's and the don'ts. It allows readers to have insights of what is expected of both management and employees.

It is meant to be a teaching tool which educators, trainers and facilitators should find extremely useful in aiding the understanding of students.

This text is ideally suited to be used by students attending Secondary or High School, undergraduate students at Colleges, Universities and Labour Colleges, and those participating in in-house orientation workplace training programmes.

It is expected that readers will find this book both user friendly and easy reading.

Dennis de Peiza
Author

CHAPTER 1   The Significance of Industrial Relations

The practice of Industrial Relations is founded on promoting the principles of natural justice, good conscience and fairness. The Industrial Relations practice which takes place at the level of the workplace, is about the engagement and relationship between the employer and employees; and the trade union as the representative of the workers / employees.

The process of collective bargaining is a key mechanism which is used in the industrial relations process. It is primarily used to negotiate employees' working conditions, wages and salaries, and to address grievances of employees. It also serves the purpose of developing a proper communication system between the employer and employees, promoting training so as to lend to the enhancement of skills, competencies and the professional development of employees. In addition, it concentrates on sensitizing employees of their contribution to the nation's economic development by way of their work ethic and productivity at work. It therefore follows that industrial relations promotes both efficiency and prosperity. In this way it contributes to both growth and development.

The practice of Industrial Relations gives rise to what is known as industrial democracy. Industrial democracy is defined as an arrangement which involves workers making decisions, sharing responsibilities and authority in the workplace. It involves the use of collective bargaining to settle problems, in which there is an expectation of mutual co-operation that leads to the reaching of an agreement.

The fact that co-operation emerges as an integral element in workplace relations, this in itself lends to the expression of a greater level of worker satisfaction. It certainly has the effect of ensuring that there is optimum use of limited and scarce resources. It is this type of congenial working environment that creates a feeling of belonging on the part of employees. This in turn helps to reduce the incidence of grievances and matters of dispute.

There are a number of other positives that are associated with the practice of industrial relations. First and foremost, it contributes to good communication between the employer and employee, and contributes to a reduction and turn over in staff. It promotes the observance of procedures, practices and processes which have been established. Most of all, it discourages unfair practices on the part of the management and the trade union as the representative of the employees. This creates the way for a non adversarial environment, and so gives way to greater collaboration, dialogue and consultation. It primarily lends to the involvement of employees in the decision making process. The significance of this development is that it allows for change to be facilitated, team work to be encouraged and innovation to be driven.

Poor industrial relations results primarily because of the intolerable attitude and contempt shown by the employer / management towards workers. This is coupled with the mental inertia that exists within the psyche of both management and labour. Other contributing factors to poor industrial relations include unfair labour practices. These include victimization and the discrimination of employees, wrongful or unfair dismissal of employees, unhealthy working conditions, lack of proper human relations, poor leadership and management skills on the part of supervisors and management personnel, unduly heavy workloads, inadequate welfare and / or social security benefits, failure on the part of management to respond to the workers' demand for wages and salaries increases, disputes over the sharing of productivity gains, retrenchment, layoffs, dismissal of workers and the lock out of employees by the employer.

Added to these is the response by workers to what is seen as the inappropriate introduction of technology in the workplace, which is often viewed as a replacement for labour. It is however the existing general economic and political climate which contributes to inflation / rising prices, wage freezes and layoffs that create much tension.

Given the pros and cons of the practice of industrial relations, nothing stands out more prominently than the fact that it promotes the enactment of sound labour legislation that is directed at protecting the welfare of workers.

The Existence of Trade Unions

The perception that the existence of trade unions is under threat is one which continues to be touted in the media and elsewhere. It would seem that this has become a strategy and plan of action, if for no other reason, is calculated to place pressure on the leadership of the labour movement. It may be that this strategy is meant to create division where possible, and moreover, to place doubts in the minds of the workforce community about the credibility of the labour movement, and its ability to serve and protect their interest.

If there is any substance to this, then it seems that those who project the idea of denouncing the labour movement and its relevancy, are certainly rather ignorant of the fact that there will always be a place for labour within an economy and society. Historically, government, labour and capital have all worked together. Further, they experience a level of dependency of each other. It has always been the case that divide and rule tactics have infiltrated the partnership. From all indications these efforts have mainly been directed at labour, so as to restrict or negate any advantages it appeared to have gained.

The bottom-line is that the net effect of these ongoing viral attempts is to erode the confidence of workers, and to create a problem for trade unions in the recruitment of members and maintaining trade union solidarity. This was lost upon the German social philosopher **Karl Marx**, as is reflected in his reminder to workers, through one of his many famous quotes. *"Workers of the world unite, you have nothing to lose but your chains."*

Democratic societies around the world acknowledge the existence of trade unions. The 185 member countries of the International Labour Organization bear testimony to this, as this body recognizes tripartite delegations, comprising of government representatives, a workers' and employers' delegate to its Annual Labour Conference. What then is the perceived threat to the existence of trade unions? Is it self-imposed, or, is it a matter of a resurgence of the dominance in capitalism in a new form, or the hypocrisy of political parties who seek to embrace trade unions for the purpose of infiltrating them in order to press their own political agendas.

It is here where vigilance, shrewd and effective leadership and management within the labour movement become paramount. There is no place for individualism, disunity and / or a fracture of the movement. Trade union solidarity must become more than a buzz word. It should be the norm and practice. Moving away from this is one sure way to kill the effectiveness of the labour movement and to expose any vulnerability there is to the elements. Any disunity or fracture within the trade union movement, would allow a government with a hidden agenda and capital to escape the watchful eye of trade unions.

The English speaking Caribbean has had a long history of a strong and vibrant labour movement, ranging from Jamaica in the north to Guyana in the south. Barbados has been exceptional, as the labour movement there has progressed to the point of being a trend setter in global industrial relations practice. It is now well known for its Social Partnership Model, which promotes the practice of social dialogue, consultation and collaboration.

The commitment to this by the social partners of government, labour and capital, would tend to suggest that any perceived threat to the existence of labour is only transitional based on the existing circumstances.

It is well known that there are phases of life in which there are seemingly insurmountable challenges. It does not mean that this is a death nail signal. It requires an identification of the besetting problem(s), and the finding of early solutions. To achieve this, a united labour movement remains the immediate answer.

Trade Union Recognition

In countries like Barbados, where the voluntarism in industrial relations is practiced, it allows for a relationship to exist between the employer and the trade union. Here, the employer voluntarily recognises the union, and the parties relate to each other without recourse to any legal procedures. As a consequence of this, workers through their trade unions and staff associations engaged the employer or the employer's organization in determining the terms and conditions of their relationship.

The culture is to build a relationship that is driven by the recognition of customs and practice and not by the force of law. The process starts with the recognition of trade unions. This requires the existence of a bargaining unit at the workplace. Under the Constitution of Barbados, every citizen enjoys freedom of association. With this being the case, the individual has the right to join a trade union of choice, or not, as he / she may determine.

The basis for the relationship and engagement between the employer and the trade union as the workers' representative, is the establishment of what is known as a bargaining unit. Here in lies the challenge, as it requires 50+1 of the employees to be members of the trade union, if a bargaining unit is to be established and the trade union is to be recognized by the employer as the bargaining agent for the employees.

Should the employer fail to recognize the trade union as the bargaining agent, then this jeopardizes the existence of the collective bargaining unit. The importance of the collective bargaining unit, resides in the fact that it supports the establishment of the negotiation process, whereby the trade union engages the employer on the terms and conditions of work of the employees; inclusive of pay. Where there is trade union recognition, it follows that the collective bargaining process should be engaged as a matter of course.

Contracts formed are binding in honour only, as they are not enforceable by law. There are no legally defined processes and procedures or issues for negotiation. The resulting collective agreement tends to cover four main areas, which are wages, hours and standard of work, contract implementation procedures and a grievance and disciplinary procedure.

In other parts of the Caribbean where Industrial Courts have been established such as Trinidad & Tobago, Guyana and the Bahamas, statutory trade union applies. This means that trade union recognition is enforceable by law. For example, if a trade union finds difficulty in arriving at a voluntary recognition agreement with an employer, the trade union reserves the right to make an application to the Industrial Court for statutory recognition.

In Barbados where an issue over voluntary trade union recognition, is referred to the Chief Labour Officer, his role is to mediate in the process.

History will however recall that in 1997, there was the matter of recognition between the Barbados Workers' Union and Royal Westmoreland Ltd. The company denied the recognition on the grounds that the union did not have the majority membership. After nine days of union action, the matter of recognition was resolved through the intervention of a private citizen. Neither party had called on the Chief Labour Officer to offer conciliation. The company agreed to reinstate terminated workers and to recognize the union as the bargaining agent for the workers.

There was also the case of Offshore Keyboarding, which was located in the Harbour Industrial Estate. This company refused to recognise the Barbados Workers' Union as the bargaining agent. The management challenged the survey method that has been entrenched as custom and practice in Barbados. The company wanted the use of a secret ballot. All elements of the Social Partners in Barbados affirmed the custom and practice as exists and admonished the company to comply. The company refused and eventually withdrew from Barbados.

Where a matter of dispute on trade union recognition is drawn to the attention of the Chief Labour Officer, the following process is to be engaged:

On receipt of the claim for recognition by a Union, the employer requests the Labour Department to conduct a survey. The Labour

Department then contacts the employer requesting the employer to provide the list of employees in the categories in which the Union is seeking recognition. Where the employer does not make the request, the Union may do so, or the Labour Department, of its own motion may request compliance of the employer. This list should correspond to the payroll list and employee classification.

Once the list of employees who are seeking unionization is received, the Labour Department notifies the Union and arranges a meeting at its premises. The totality of the Union's list, which is always in card form, is presented by the Union. The list provided by the Union constitutes the bona fide/signed up membership of employees of the particular enterprise.

All members and officials associated with that Union are then requested to leave the room so as to provide absolute privacy to the Labour Officers who are conducting the survey.

The Union's list is then checked and purged for any anomalies or inconsistencies such as:

(i) Whether an employee's name on the list provided by the company checks out or matches those on Union's list;

(ii) Whether there are membership signatures after the effective date of recognition claim by Union;

(iii) Whether the numbers tally, either by category or overall.

Any anomalies or unusual findings are noted for study, or, query, or, explanation by either party, when thought necessary.

Additionally, the Union's list is then checked off by matching against the employer's list and the numbers are recorded.

A record is made and both parties are informed as to the numbers in the findings.

Bearing in mind that Barbados has ratified the ILO Convention #87, Concerning Freedom of Association and Protection of the Right to Organize, the trade union by seeking recognition is attempting to ensure that workers access the right to which they are entitled.

The Right To Be Unionized

The Constitution of Barbados is similar to that of other countries of the British Commonwealth. It promotes freedom of association as a fundamental human right. It is a fact that in most Commonwealth countries the right to unionization is guaranteed under law.

As a consequence of this, every citizen and resident has the right to join or not to join a trade union. This is not to be challenged, as the decision to associate rests with the choice and preference of the individual. Those who opt not to join a trade union should not be subjected to ridicule, should not be discriminated against, or, ostracized.

It is however a matter of concern when persons are denied the right to be unionized. It is known that some employers would not encourage their employees to be unionized. This is particularly distressing, since it is perceived that those in an enterprise who opt to hold membership in a trade union are sometimes apparently targeted. It is believed that in many instances, such persons are unceremoniously terminated by the employer, or are placed under extreme pressure in their daily work life; to the point that they sometimes opt to 'cash in' the job.

In either instance, this is neither a desirable nor an appropriate thing to happen. It is to be emphasized that any fears or reservations which workers may have about joining a union ought to be dispelled, since it is their right to be unionized. Moreover, they should be comforted by the fact that they are not to be disadvantaged because they are members of a trade union. Therefore, they should see unionization as their life line to representation at the workplace.

All employees should be conscious of the fact that it is their right to be a member of trade union of their choice, to decide to leave or remain a member of a trade union; even if it is different from the one which is recognized by the employer; and moreover, to belong to more than one trade union. Employees should be aware that they cannot be refused employment, unfairly treated at work, harassed, dismissed or selected for redundancy because they are members of a union, or have expressed an intention to join a union.

Employers on the other hand should be weary of their actions as these could put them on the wrong side of the law. Employers ought to be reminded that ignorance of the law is not an acceptable excuse.

As it pertains to foreign or international enterprises looking to establish companies within countries outside of their home base, the owners / management of these companies should become familiar with the existing labour laws, customs and practices of the particular country they intend to operate in.

Workers' Rights

Every employee has basic human rights and rights at work. These rights obtain irrespective of the status of the employee as a unionized or, non-unionized member. The basic human rights of workers are embodied in the rights at work. These are: The right to freedom of speech and association, the right to non discriminatory treatment, the right to a fair trial (The right to due process in the workplace) and the right to peaceful assembly.

The Declaration on Fundamental Principles and Rights at Work which were adopted in 1998 by the 86th Annual Conference of the International Labour Organization (ILO), identifies eight core conventions. The Declaration covers four Fundamental Principles and Rights at Work. These are freedom of association and the effective recognition of the right to collective bargaining, the elimination of all forms of forced or compulsory labour, the effective abolition of child labour and the elimination of discrimination in respect to employment and occupation.

Freedom to join a union - Bargaining Collectively and to take Action: Freedom of Association and Protection of the Right to Organize, Convention,1948, No 87, Right to Organize and Collective Bargaining, Convention 1951, No. 98

Abolition of Force Labour:
Forced Labour Convention, 1930, No.29,   Abolition of Force Labour Convention, 1957, No 105

Abolition of labour by children before the end of compulsory school age: Minimum Age Convention, No 138, Worst Forms of Child Labour Convention, 1999, No 182

No discrimination at work:
Equal Remuneration Convention, 1951, No.10, Discrimination (Employment and Occupation) Convention, 1958, No 111

Workers have a right to join a trade union, not to be refused a job, dismissed, harassed, or selected for redundancy simply because they are a member of, or wish to join a trade union.

As a member of a recognized trade union, a worker has the right to take part in trade union activities both within and outside the employee's normal working hours or at a time agreed with the employer.

An employee is to be paid for participation in union activities, inclusive of attendance to training courses, workshops and seminars. This does not apply in the instance of protest actions such as strikes, and picketing, where the employees are not on the job.

The Shop Steward as the workers' representative at the workplace, has the right to carry out the assigned duties without interference. The Shop Steward is the voice of the workers at the workplace, and is therefore the frontline representative of his / her coworkers.

An employee has a right to withdraw or withhold his/her labour, but does not have the right to be paid on withholding of his / her labour, unless otherwise stated in the contract of employment.

Employees should not be subjected to victimization or discrimination in any form by their employer. It is unlawful for an employer to attempt to discipline an employee who is carrying out legitimate trade union duties at an appropriate time. An employee who is subjected to being disciplined on account of those activities, is deemed to have been victimized and / or discriminated against.

The basic rights of an employee are:
- To be paid a wage or salary
- The right to be unionized
- Employer to provide a safe working environment
- To have the employer provide tools and equipment to do the job
- The employee is not to be held responsible for any losses incurred while performing legitimate work on the behalf of the employer.

Occupational Safety & Health
Responsibilities of the Employer and Employee

The international standards on Occupational Safety and Health are guided by the International Labour Organization Convention on Occupational Safety and Health, C i55, 1981.

Countries such as Barbados which have ratified the Convention, have subsequently passed legislation to guide safety and health policies, practices, procedures and processes within the workplace.

For instance, the provisions of the Safety and Health Act (SHaW Act) of Barbados, serve to protect both the interest of the employee and the employer. The Act therefore imposes shared responsibility on both the employer and employee to ensure workplace best practices and standards are observed. None the less, there is an overarching responsibility placed on employers to provide and maintain a safe working environment. Employers have a duty to provide a safe place of work, a safe system of work, safe tools, safe fellow employees and adequate supervision and training. They are also required to:.

- Provide a workplace free from recognized hazards
- Provide and use means to make the workplace safe
- Prohibit employees from entering, or being in any workplace that is not safe
- Construct the workplace so that it is safe
- Prohibit alcohol and narcotics from the workplace
- Provide information, instruction, training and supervision as is necessary to ensure the health and safety of employees
- Prohibit employees from using tools and equipment that are not safe
- Establish, supervise and enforce rules that lead to a safe and healthy work environment that are effective in the workplace
- Control the use of chemical agents
- Protect employees from biological agents

Employees have a responsibility to:

- To play an active role in creating a safe and healthy workplace and to comply with all safety and health rules.
- Study and follow all safe practices that apply to their work
- Coordinate and cooperate with all other employees in the workplace to eliminate on the job injuries and illnesses
- Be encouraged to apply the principles of accident prevention in their daily work and use proper safety devices and protective equipment as required by their employment or employer
- Take care of all protective equipment properly
- Not to wear torn or loose clothing while working around machinery
- Report promptly to their supervisor every industrial injury or occupational illness
- Not to remove, displace, damage, or destroy or carry off any safe guard, notice or warning provided to make the workplace safe
- Not to interfere with the use of any safe guard by anyone in the workplace
- Not to interfere with the use of any work practice designed to protect them from injury

- Do everything reasonably necessary to protect the life and safety of fellow employees;
- Report a job related injury or illness to the employer and seek to prompt treatment;
- Ensure reportable accidents and cases of occupational diseases are reported by the employer to the Chief Labour Officer;
- Be familiar with applicable workplace rules, laws and regulations relating to occupational safety and health;
- Stand for membership and participation in the safety committee;
- Cooperate fully with the employer in measures intended to promote occupational safety and health;
- Use personal protective equipment (PPE) as prescribed;
- Report hazardous conditions to the employer;
- Take reasonable action within their capability to eliminate workplace hazards;
- Co-operate with the Factory Inspector on the occasions of visits to the workplace;
- Comply with applicable rules, laws and regulations relating to occupational safety and health; and;
- Exercise all workplace rights in a reasonable manner and pursue responsibilities with diligence.

The perspective of the International Labour Organization (ILO) on the promotion of Safety and Health at Work is as follows:

The safe work programme is aimed at creating nationwide awareness of the dimensions and consequences of work related accidents, injuries and diseases. It promotes the goal of basic protection for all workers in conformity with international labour standards, and the design implementation of effective preventative policy programmes.

CHAPTER 2　　　　　　　　Job Recruitment

Finding a job in today's contracting job market can be both a challenging and frustrating experience. The average job seeker is forced to face fierce competition from those who have the required job qualifications and skills; and in some cases, the work experience.

Both qualifications and work experience are important, but it is not always the case that one overrides the other. The decision as to which of the two is given priority in the recruitment process, rest entirely with the employer. It may be argued that some employers consider that work experience matters most. While there is merit in this, it does not necessary follow that this will automatically make a difference in the level of the employee's performance. Additionally, it provides a measure of comfort for the employer that the employee has the requisite knowledge. It has long been accepted that the individual who holds certification from a reputable education or training institution, is in a better position to satisfy a prospective employer of his /her knowledge base, competence and skill level.

Studies have shown, that there are some individuals who possess the requisite qualification for the job, but who unfortunately fall woefully short of the skills necessary to effectively play the role that is required. This is one of the shortcomings that the job interview process throws up. It is those individuals who have the ability to handle the interview process better than most that get the nod over their competitors. They simply have the ability to be articulate and convincing. The argument has been made that placing the primary emphasis on the interview process is flawed and needs to be re-examined. While the interviewing process used for the recruitment of employees might be called into question, arguments posed against it may be countered by the view that it is the fairest system of all.

One is left to ponder—*'What are the solutions if any?'* If the playing field is to be level, then it should demand that persons, who are applying for a job vacancy or even a promotional opportunity, should ensure that at least, they have the minimum requirements for the job. There is no basis on which the applicant can cry foul if the individual fails to meet the basic requirements or expectations.

To get around this, it is best that individuals make an early decision with regards to their intended career path, and pursue both educational and training programmes that equip them for the vocation of choice. It is not always possible that an individual may find a suitable job in the specific area of training, and for which they were educated. This is where the benefit of cross training or being multi skilled has its place. Today, the job market demands that employees are multi skilled. This is certainly one way for individuals to ensure that they stay ahead of the competition.

Employers are more likely to employ an individual who brings a sound knowledge base and a variety of skills and talents to the table. This is where the argument of experience becomes a talking point. Nothing can and will ever beat experience. However, if experience is all that counts, it certainly reduces the importance that is to be attached to the knowledge factor.

The contention can be made that most employers who are concerned with developing and enhancing their business, are most likely to search for prospective employees who have the knowledge and skills, and are trainable to do the job. Using on the job training as a means to an end, today's employers are expected to be more supportive of apprenticeship or job attachment programmes. The support for these schemes, rest with the understanding that such engagement allows them the opportunity to assess the individual. Based on a good performance report, the employer can exercise the option of offering full time employment, or engagement on a contract basis. This approach may also be seen as a cost effective measure.

Job recruitment is not necessary an easy task. With the advent of globalization, it might have become more difficult, as globalization has opened up the door for the recruitment of workers from any part of the world. Prospective employees now have to face up to stiffer competition, as employers look to recruit the most suitably qualified, trained and in some instances, those with requisite job experience.

Those entering the job market for the first time face the greatest degree of difficulty. The world of work now demands a highly trained and skilled employee, and so for those who are coming directly from university and college, who have academic qualification, now have to concern themselves as to whether they meet the expectations of today's employer.

In the specialized fields such as accounting and or nursing, it may appear that the challenge faced in finding employment might not be as difficult. Given the saturation of employment opportunities in some professionals, and the fact that employers are driven to recruit the 'cream of the crop', many job seekers can find themselves stuck on the unemployment list.

Employers at all times will have the final say in the recruitment process. They set out the criteria which is to be used in selecting the most suitable applicant. In the recruitment process, the applicant has the opportunity to market himself or herself to the prospective employer. While the prospective employer has a profile in mind to determine if an interviewee will be the right fit to the organization, the applicant also expects that a fair and transparent process will be followed. The fact that this will be guided by an objective criterion will make job recruitment a less challenging exercise.

A JOB vs. A CAREER

A career means engaging in the same type of work for one's working life. A job is described as a piece of work or a specific task that is undertaken as part of the routine of the occupation of an individual.

A job maybe full time or part time, temporary or seasonal. Individuals are also contracted to work for a specific time period to complete a specific task.

Self-employed workers are persons who work for themselves as opposed to being an employee of another business. Self-employed persons offer services to customers and clients, and so generate their own income.

There is also a type of work which is known as *'Moonlighting.'* This is the practice where an individual works in another job or jobs, in addition to one's main job, usually to earn extra income. Persons, who engage in this practice, usually do so outside of, or, after their regular hours of work. This could either be in the day or night.

There is a distinct difference between a job and a career. A job is described as a one-time event, where as a career is a lifelong process. The common thread which can be identified in a job and a career, is that they both have expectations and obligations attached. These are commonly referred to as duties and responsibilities.

Inasmuch that a career is the pursuit of a long life ambition, it requires a good education background, training and work experience. It is generally expected that a career person is qualified to do the job he is doing.

In both a job and a career, the individual receives payment for the services rendered. However, when a person undertakes a job, it is simply for the purpose of earning money. The career person has a focus on employment opportunities that have a significant bearing on the individual's future career. This allows for upward mobility along the chosen career path.

It is however easier for a person to do several different jobs and work for different employers during the life of his career. An example of this, is a medical doctor who may have his / her own private practice, but yet works at one or more hospitals and other private clinics.

Starting a New Job

When starting a new job, the individual should commence work with a positive mind set. The individual should concentrate on how to make a positive difference in the workplace. Creating a good first and lasting impression, projecting a positive image and being a team player should be the three things that matter most.

Creating First and Lasting Impressions
- Project a positive Image / Exhibit self-confidence;
- Exhibit the skills required of the professional business person;
- Positive body language and posture;
- Adopt a business dress code;
- Communication: Pay attention to speech and deportment;
- Display good business etiquette;
- Avoid office gossip and politicking

Projecting a Positive Image
- Have an open communication channel;
- Remove any barriers to communication;
- Develop listening skills;
- Be courteous;
- Behave like an adult;
- Pay attention to your values and credibility;
- Be conscious of the Vision, Mission and Values of your organization.

Delegating Tasks
- Motivate yourself and others;
- Take ownership for any task delegated to you;
- Build trust;

Be a Team Player
- Demonstrate the qualities of an excellent team;
- Analyze your team;
- Make sure each team member knows his/her responsibilities;
- Be able to deal with team conflict;
- Accept constructive criticism.

How to stand out as an Employee

In order to be effective, and deemed as an outstanding employee, involves a combination of measures / strategies. It involves the employee asserting good personal values, work ethics, while at the same time observing and adhering to the organization's standards and practices.

Listed below are some of the strategies/factors that will ensure that you will be noticed in the workplace:

- Understanding and learning the job
- Understanding the culture of the workplace
- Following company rules
- Being productive
- Being responsible
- Finding ways to impress the boss
- Displaying a good work attitude
- Bonding with other co-workers
- Coping and manage stress
- Being able to resolve conflict
- Being assertive
- Being co-operative
- Learning from your mistakes
- Upholding of the company's image
- Exceeding employee expectations
- Taking pride in your work
- Managing criticism
- Demonstrating the ability to listen
- Dealing with difficult people and situations
- Making work meaningful and enjoyable
- Making a difference at work by taking initiative
- Coping with work and domestic life
- Good time management
- Being multi-faceted
- Being results oriented.

Interviewing Techniques

Below are some guidelines that should be followed when you have been invited to attend an interview.

Do's:
- ❒ Be sincere and direct
- ❒ Be attentive and polite
- ❒ Ask relevant questions
- ❒ Answer questions concisely
- ❒ Use specific examples to illustrate points
- ❒ Use standard English

Don't:
- ❒ Smoke
- ❒ Chew
- ❒ Try to control the entire interview
- ❒ Bring up salary, benefits or working hours
- ❒ Be too serious
- ❒ Let your depression or discouragement show
- ❒ Make negative comments about anyone or anything, including former employers
- ❒ Look at your watch
- ❒ Take extensive notes

Women:
- ❒ Extremely long or uncut nails are a real turnoff. Your nails should be well groomed and neat.
- ❒ Don't wear more than two rings per hand or one earring in each ear.
- ❒ No face jewelry or ankle bracelets should be worn.
- ❒ Wear stockings. Bare legs should be avoided.
- ❒ Opened or backless shoes and slippers should never be worn.
- ❒ Don't wear leather jackets
- ❒ All visible tattoos should be covered

Men:
- ❒ Men's jackets are to be full-body and looser rather than fitted or tight.
- ❒ Don't wear leather jackets.
- ❒ The wearing of a collared shirt and tie is preferable.
- ❒ Reframe from wearing excessive jewelry
- ❒ Be properly groomed
- ❒ Remove all visible body piercing jewelry

The Contract of Employment

The employment contract is a legal agreement entered into between two parties (i.e. the individual and the employer).

It is the employee's responsibility to ensure that the conditions of the contract meet with his / her expectations and satisfaction before signing off.

What to look for and consider before signing off on the Contract of Employment?

Here are some of the basic issues that ought to be carefully considered before signing off.

Type of Contract of Employment
(a) Temporary / Probationary
(b) Permanent
(c) Fixed period. (i.e. There is a starting and terminal date)
(d) Intermediary – Seasonal Contracts
Is the contract for, or of service?

Hours of Work
The contract needs to identify your specific hours of work for example (8:00a.m. - 4:00p.m.) or (9:00a.m. - 5:00p.m.)

Conditions of Work
What compensation is given for overtime work?

Is it the practice to pay time and half pay for overtime work during the work week, and double time on weekends and public holidays?

Is time in lieu of pay given?

Avoid the possibility of being exploited where the employer requires you to work on Saturdays and Public holidays on your off day, without offering the appropriate compensation.

Prospective employees should establish whether there is a shift system of work and how it is regulated. They should find out what conditions apply to employees who are required to work unconscionable hours. An example of this would be with respect to those employees who are required to commence or end work during hours when there is no scheduled bus service i.e. public transport. In most Caribbean territories there is no twenty-four hour bus service. The employer should therefore put in place suitable arrangements for transportation to ensure that staff can arrive and depart from work safely.

Place of Work
The place of work should be clearly established.
The employee should be aware if a transfer policy exists and how it is exercised.

Benefits

Prospective employees should ensure that they are aware of what benefits are being offered by the organization and should seek information on the following:

Does the company offer an Employee Pension Plan?

What are the terms of the plan?
What is the employer's contribution to the plan?

Will the employee lose the benefits of the Group Life and Health Plan if employment is terminated or if the employee resigns from the company?

Do you still retain membership under the plan or if it is transferrable?

Annual Holiday

Does the annual holiday of three weeks for one for 1-4 years of employment and four weeks for five years of employment and over, applies as in the case of the Labour Laws of Barbados?

Annual Pay Increase

The contract needs to identify how this is determined. Is there an incremental % increase in salary, or are there negotiated pay increases every two or three years?

Reporting

The contract should identify the person to whom you are expected to report.

This is to avoid any issues as to who is your reporting officer.

Promotional Opportunities

The contract should also identify promotional opportunities and eligibility for the same.

Job Description

This should be set out in writing. It should address the employee's role and functions.
Any changes to the job descriptions are to be discussed with the employer and employee / or trade union as the representative body of the workers; and **mutually agreed upon**.

Performance Standards

Reference should be made to the company's Procedures or Operations Manual. This is sometimes referred to as the Employees' Handbook.

Annual Performance Review

Employees should be aware of whether the company uses an Annual Performance Review to assess performance. They should know who carries out the appraisal, at what time this is done during the work year, and what are the areas which are to be specifically addressed in the review process.

Leave
Employees ought to establish if the company makes provision for study leave, training leave, compassionate leave, maternity and paternity leave.
Compassionate leave is granted when there is a family bereavement.
Paternity leave is a time given to a father when there is a new born in the family.

Training and Retraining
Does the enterprise or organization provides opportunity for training and retraining?
How is any training and retraining applied towards internal promotion?

Discipline
Have a clear understanding of the established disciplinary procedure.
Ascertain if there is a 'No Tolerance Policy' of the enterprise/ organization and what is it.

Exit Clause
The contract should give some indication of how it can be terminated by either party.

Workplace Etiquette

Standard Workplace Etiquette
- Punctuality
- Dress Appropriately
- Stay away from gossip
- Greet everyone politely
- Respect People (religion, opinions)
- Respect your seniors and colleagues
- Avoid wearing strongly scented products (perfumes, deodorants)
- Be sociable
- Avoid telling jokes that could be considered offensive or sensitive
- Seek to discuss and solve problems
- Avoid speaking loudly
- Conduct yourself appropriately
- Be very careful while interacting with the other employees and especially with female employees
- Avoid intimate relationships

Breaches of Workplace Etiquette
- Cursing
- Excessive workplace gossip
- Drinking on the job
- Leaving without telling anyone / without permission
- Abuse of personal telephone calls
- Eating someone else's food from the fridge
- Bad hygiene
- Personal bad habits
- Wasting resources

Use of Cellular Phone, Business Phones and Emails at Work
- Cell phones are disruptive. Avoid the use of cell phones particularly on your employers' time.
- You should use good and grammatically correct language while writing e-mails.
- While talking to your seniors or juniors on the telephone, be polite and listen to what they are saying carefully.
- Answer phone calls and e-mails in a timely manner.
- Do not conduct your personal business during office hours.
- There are some companies, particularly international companies where the use of cell phones or personal phone calls are not allowed.

Social Networking
- Limit your social activities in the virtual world, while you are at work.

Dressing Appropriately for Work

When one speaks of a dress code, reference is being made to a determined standard of dress. The purpose of the dress code is to uphold the professional image of an organization and its members. A dress code carries built in rules or signals, which are meant to convey a message by the person wearing the clothing. Interestingly enough, the message that is intended to be conveyed is largely dependent on how the clothing is worn. This speaks largely to what is determined as the standard of dress that each employee in any given organization is expected to observe.

According to Susan Heathfield, a Human Resources expert in the United States of America, "A dress code is a set of standards that companies develop to help provide their employees with guidance about what is appropriate to wear to work. Dress codes range from formal to business casual to casual. The formality of the workplace dress code is normally determined by the amount of interaction employees have with customers or clients." This definition should clearly suggest to readers that there is 'no one size fit all' approach that may be applied with respect to what a dress code should be. It clearly has its place in what is appropriate for the time and place, and the nature of the job.

For employees who are in a position to directly interface with members of the public, attention ought to be paid to the appropriateness of their attire, and the manner in which it is worn.

Every individual in seeking to comply with the standard should be driven by the need to carry himself/herself in a manner that reflects that the individual is taking pride in one's appearance. If this is lacking, then it is likely that the individual could suffer from a low self image and poor self esteem. These invariably can have an impact on that individual's morale, work ethic and productivity. These set of circumstances could easily be the catalyst for a nightmare for management, as the possibility exists that both work colleagues and customers might experience relations and communication difficulties in their dealing with the employee.

As referred to earlier, the standard of dress does much to enhance the image of the organization. It is therefore for every workplace to clearly set out the guidelines to be followed. This is important in order to avoid any interpretation of the workplace dress code(s). Where the dress code lends itself to interpretation by individuals, it opens the way to diversity and subjectivity. A good example of this is the dress code set for teachers in the Barbados Public Schools. The regulation refers to teachers being 'Soberly Dress.' What is soberly dress can be the subject of an extensive debate. It is however reasonable to conclude that where the offending party has gone to ridiculous lengths, then the grounds for disciplinary action are justifiable. Beyond that, it would seem that the debate will remain a contentious one.

Having drawn attention to the importance to dress standards at work, it is important to take this a step further and urge that persons reframe from being outlandish in their mode of dress. From the trends that can be observed in the mode of dress, it would appear that in some instances, females in particular go overboard. There are some workplaces that are becoming the stage for fashion parades, and judging from the makeup artistry, places of beauty contests.

The dress standards go from one extreme to another. By the same token, both males and females are often guilty of bordering on the sublime. Females in particular seem to find pleasure in revealing body parts. Men have gradually moved away from the low waist pants, but instead have joined their female counterparts in the wearing of tattoos and ear rings. The unanswered question is—'What's next, and when will it stop?'

To all and sundry the call is to wear appropriate clothing to work, even if it's business casual. You may consider not wearing strong cologne or perfume to work. Most importantly, take care of personal hygiene.

CHAPTER 3 Team Building

There are fundamental differences which distinguish a team from a group. A team is defined as a group of people working together for a common goal. Success is measured. Each team member has a role and function. A team can involve as few as two people. A team is not a mere aggregate of individuals. A team's success depends on the interdependent and collective efforts of various team members. Team members are likely to have significant impacts on one another as they work together.

In sharp contrast, a group is defined as a combination of people who have a common interest. It therefore is composed of people who recognize each other as members of their group and can distinguish these individuals from nonmembers.

Purpose & Importance of Team Building

It is expected that in a team-oriented environment that all members of the organization / enterprise will work together in an effort to help the organization to produce results and achieve success; through the attainment of the goals and targets set.

In team building it is expected that all members would be acquainted with the mission and vision of the organization, and of what it wants to achieve. Without the knowledge of these expectations and a clear understanding of the strategies to be employed towards achieving the desired results, the possibility exists that the goals, aims and objectives may not be realized. Commitment to the organization therefore becomes an important factor if it is to achieve its goals.

Developing A Culture of Team Work

The culture of team work is nurtured in an environment where there is collaboration and cooperation. It is expected that the environment would be predisposed to encouraging thinking, planning, decision making, the building of trust and openness, and the practice of good human and interpersonal relations.

Team building will more than likely be driven in an environment where employees are motivated. The environment should enable employees to enjoy good working conditions, a range of benefits and security of tenure. Employee recognition, regard for the professional and personal development of employees, opportunities for advancement and promotion, and the fact that work can be made interesting and rewarding, will contribute to cementing a culture of team work.

The importance of motivation is supported by Frederick Herzberg: *Motivation-Hygiene Theory*. He opined that 'Motivation factors aren't necessarily expected, but when they're in place, they produce feelings of satisfaction and drive employees to succeed.(**The Motivation to Work, 1959**).

Marcelino Sanchez in his work 'Keys to Building a Strong Team or Organizational Culture,' identified three critical factors on which a productive team is built. In doing so he opined:

"My thoughts on building a productive team culture (subculture). For a team to do what it needs to do in a way that they like to do it and be effective, they have to develop certain norms of behavior. Norms of behavior are a function of many things but three critical factors are:

1. Leadership – how the team leader leads and interacts with others (in the team).

2. Values / beliefs held by the team – most teams have ground rules but they rarely make a difference because they are task oriented (be on time, don't interrupt, etc.) and only written on a flipchart page. Mutually espoused values and beliefs have to be written on individuals' minds and hearts.

3. Consequences – a well defined accountability process is necessary to reinforce desired behaviors and attitudes."

Key Characteristics of Team Building

It must be reemphasized that the role played by each member of the team is vital to the success of the organization. It is therefore expected that each member of the team is required to contribute to ensuring that the targets set are achieved. Failing this, the overall success to be attained can be undermined in the absence of the collective effort. It is expected that there will be a high level of interdependence amongst team members. For a team to be effective, it requires that it has leadership. The team leader should be an individual who has good people skills and is committed to the team approach.

Communication stands out as a important factor in team building. It effectiveness is best recorded within a relaxed environment, where information sharing and participation of individuals is the norm. A good communication system and practices will contribute to the buy in by of employees, where they have a clear understanding of the goals, targets and objectives of the organization. Most importantly it helps to develop trust amongst the members of the organization.

Defining the role of each team member is necessary. This would help team members to know how they can influence the team's agenda, and make a valuable contribution without fear or malice. In the case of the latter, it is expected that the incidence of personal attacks and negative responses to criticism, will be reduced if not eliminated. Where the roles of team members are clearly defined, and the confidence, commitment, and enthusiasm of individuals in the team are high, these would lend to the team's capacity to create new ideas.

Team Ethics

These are built on the foundation of professional standards and ethical code of conduct, the existence of a corporate culture, corporate policies and procedures, and personal and team values.

Applying Universal Ethical Principles in the Workplace

In the workplace there is the expectation that management will undertake to apply standards which reflect that it accords with universal ethical principles that underpins its behavior and relationship with the internal customers, the employees, and the external customers in the public that the organization serves.

For a harmonious working relationship to exist in the workplace, the manager has to first demonstrate a respect for people. Added to this is the recognition that people are to be treated fairly. This means that they are not to be discriminated against, abused or exploited. It logically follows that there should be respect for the observance for equity and justice.

Inasmuch that justice is concerned with power sharing and preventing the abuse of power, it becomes imperative that management moves to embrace workers in working to achieve full worker participation, and the ultimate of collective responsibility.

Successful and effective managers rarely lose sight of the fact that people are the most valuable resource of any organization. It is against the backdrop of this the realization emerges that people should be treated as individuals with rights to be honoured and defended, who have both a personal and professional responsibility.

It is therefore important to relate to the fact that the principle of taking personal and professional responsibility, requires not only that people avoid doing harm to others but that they exhibit courteous behaviour; and in so doing, uphold the standards expected of all persons.

Such high moral standards could be exemplify by not engaging in or becoming party to such activities as fraud, embezzlement, moral turpitude, illegal drugs, or use of misleading statements.

If management is to understand its role and to have an appreciation of what is expected of it in leading a successful organization or work team, it ought not to lose sight of the core principles that guide ethical behaviour within the workplace. These are identified as values, trust, loyalty and commitment, honesty, respect for one another and avoiding conflicts of interest.

Management is therefore entrusted with the ethical responsibility of making the well being of the enterprise and its employees the basis of decision making and action. Equally so, management is expected to show respect for the civil and trade union rights of employees, undertake to execute professional responsibilities with honesty and prosperity, maintain professional relationships which that rule out vindictiveness, willful intimidation and disparagement, protect confidential information, void preferential treatment and conflict of interest.

It is essential that management seeks to honour all contracts until completion, release or dissolution by mutual agreement by all parties. It is imperative that personal politics should have no part of any business.

Most importantly, managers need to show respect for the labour code / standards and national laws governing business and employment practices.

As a genuine guide to following ethical practices in the workplace, it is essential that managers recognize and respect not only their own rights and responsibilities, but also the rights and responsibilities of other members / employees of the workplace.

Dress: Deportment & the Corporate Identity

There is an adage that says '*a man is known by the company he keeps.*' That to all intents and purposes carries a significant meaning. This can be referenced to the fact that employees who wear a uniform are easily identifiable. In earlier years, it would seem that the wearing of uniforms was limited to a group of public sector employees, which included the police, soldiers, nurses and postmen and women. With the passage of time, this has changed significantly. It has moved to the point where employees in various departments and agencies of government now wear a uniform, or alternately, display a logo on their apparel. This allows for easy identification of the place at which they work.

Within the private sector, it is almost the norm for employees to be uniformed. The wearing of the uniform which carries the logo of the company or organization, serves a promotional purpose. It projects a visual corporate image, which is intended to create easy identification of the company or organization by members of the public. This in business circles is referred to as corporate identity. Whereas having a corporate identity becomes important from a promotional point of view, its importance really lies in how the company or organization is perceived by the public.

It is for this reason that employees should be educated on the importance and significance attached to the wearing of a uniform. The wearing of a uniform with dignity and pride, and more so, with a sense of decency and responsibility, cannot be overstated. Compliance with this is basically a reflection of the hallmark of discipline within the organization. In order to maintain this level of discipline, there may be the need for constant reinforcement on maintaining standards of deportment, denouncing and punishing repeated acts of irresponsible behaviour.

The deteriorating of standards will continue to thrive in an environment where no decisive action is taken to address pockets of negligence and indifference, and where deportment is sacrificed simply because it is a matter of low priority on the enterprise or organization's agenda.

Some of the common amazing but distressing sights to behold, include seeing persons who are attired in uniform, supposedly at work, or on the way to or from work, sitting in a bar, rum shop, street corner and even in a party environment, openly drinking an alcoholic beverage, or engaging in some form of antisocial behaviour. It would appear that this has become the norm and acceptable to some.

There is a responsibility placed on employers and also trade unions representatives to discourage any form of inept deportment displayed by employees while dressed in their uniform. There ought to be a consciousness of how this could mushroom and become a trend for others to follow.

Trade unions are known to play their part in negotiating for work uniforms for employees. With this having been attained, it is left to employees to behave responsibly, and wear their uniforms with pride to uphold the company's corporate image.

Enhancing Workplace Productivity

In any discussion on workplace productivity, it is almost inevitable that the words input and output would be included; as these are considered two of the important elements in determining productivity outcomes. It is an undisputed fact that the value of inputs will impact on the outcomes that are attainable. Outcomes may be measured against the backdrop of targets set and attained, and specific goals which have been achieved. Where there is a sense of non achievement, attention is then placed on finding reasons for the shortfall.

Employers have the expectations that employees will constantly perform at a high level. It is not an unrealistic expectation provided that employers place the necessary tools at the disposal of their employees to do the job, and offer a safe and enabling working environment. Added to these would be good terms and conditions of work. There can be no denying that employees in both the public and private sectors are hard pressed to meet their employer's expectations. This is because the resources needed to complete the tasks are often lacking.

Irrespective of the human resources available, what excuse can be made for not having the necessary tools in place to help to drive and enhance the level of worker productivity? Complaints of inadequate production levels could be inextricably linked to the absence of raw materials, inefficient, or, the absence of requisite equipment, as well as the lack of proper workplace systems and accountability.

It can be surmised that the unavailability of equipment among other things could impact on the delivery of services and on a decline in the level of productivity. Those who work in the public sector sometimes face harsh criticisms for the delivery of service. Where in some cases such criticism is merited, those who are most vociferous, should also take the time to assess the causation factors, before resorting to bashing those who are only doing their best to deliver services under trying circumstances.

Factors affecting productivity include unclear objectives and priorities. This can be attributed to poor management, lack of a strategic direction and poor communication. Bound up in this, is the holding of too many meetings, the inability to make decisions and poor time management skills. Additionally, there may be too much work, a lack of requisite resources, and inflexible technology which will not support a business that is required to be flexible.

Factors influencing productivity include the knowledge and skills of personnel, motivation, user-friendly technology, operational procedures, management and labour collaboration, resources, team orientation (individual and departmental) health of personnel, rewards and compensation, and the national work ethic.

Freedom of Speech

Freedom of speech is considered to be one of the fundamental rights of people living within a democratic society. Freedom of speech has always been championed by those freedom fighters who have continuously fought struggles for the rights of people irrespective of their colour, race, creed, class, sex, religious and political beliefs or persuasions. Today the United Nations as a world body continues to champion the cause for freedom of speech, as it promotes and encourages respect for human rights and the fundamental freedoms of all without distinction as to race, sex, language or religion.

Notwithstanding that freedom of speech is accepted within a democratic society, there is nothing to say that there is any such thing as absolute freedom of speech. There are limitations to freedom of speech. These include slander, libel, defamation of one's character, the use of obscene language, and the inciting of violence so that it becomes a threat to national security and safety. Simply put, freedom of speech doesn't mean the freedom to say whatever you want and wherever you want. This means that the law of the land does impose some limitations on the behaviour of the individual.

Bound by the need to maintain decency and order, all persons in a democratic society have the right to express themselves both orally and in writing. Many may see this as a necessary evil, which is to be applied in order to protect some persons from themselves, as their utterances may fall way out of line of the accepted standards. Be this as it may, those who have the power or authority to ensure compliance, should disabuse their minds that they should or could act without giving careful consideration; and so come across that they are intended to muzzle the voices of persons.

Such behaviour is often found in workplaces where employers tend to use this intimidatory tactic to silence shop stewards and vocal employees. This is disgusting, and is even of more concern where there are signals that members of a society are left to feel uneasy, constrained and threatened by virtue of the fact that they may be victimized or sanctioned in some form or fashion for airing their views; although within the bounds of decency and order.

The citizenry of a country must not be made to feel this way. In the practice of democracy there ought to be a level playing field. Using Barbados as an example, a question may be asked—"Why should parliamentarians be afforded the luxury of so called 'absolute freedom' within the walls of the House of Assembly or the Senate where there is extended latitude to make statements sometimes that could be considered defamatory without having the fear of any action being taken against them by an ordinary citizen?" This is what can be considered a privilege.

This takes us to look at the exercise of power and authority where an employer would undertake to terminate an employee because the individual made a comment that he / she did not like the actions of his / her employer. Would such an action be considered as appalling? What would be the likely grounds for termination? In such a situation, it is possible that the employer may cite the employee for insubordination. Clearly, any thought given to termination should be based on the severity of the comments.

Since it is established that there is nothing known as absolute freedom of speech, employees may want to be mindful of what they say, the manner in which it is communicated and where it is said. It is always wise to pay attention to what is done and how it is done. It is also good practice that people think before they speak, as it is extremely difficult to remove from the receiver's lasting memory what has already been said.

In bringing balance to the assertion that there is no such thing of absolute freedom, the point must be advanced that there are necessary restrictions on freedom of speech as required by law. For example, the law will impose restrictions on employees so as to prevent them from divulging confidential information, information about a company's finances, transactions and trade secrets, contractual non-disclosure and for security purposes. A doctor whether employed by the state or as a self-employed person, is sworn to maintain the confidentiality of patient information. This also applies to the employer in any organization or enterprise as it pertains to the confidential information of an employee.

At the workplace the control over freedom of speech is useful for the purpose of prohibiting discrimination and sexual harassment. It is also worthwhile protection for the whistle-blower. Employees and employers should therefore always be aware of the fact that they don't have a constitutional right to free speech or freedom of expression at work. It is advisable that they commit to memory the old cliché of 'What is good for the goose may not be good for the gander.'

Service Excellence

The promotion of service excellence has increasingly become a talking point, as customers complain of the poor service delivered by employees. This is a matter that continues to raise its ugly head. In any country that boasts of being a service driven economy, this development is one of grave concern.

Offering good service to customers whether it is within the private sector or the public service, has to be seen as the best that can be had. It however starts with the establishment of a set of standards that management has the responsibility for developing and enforcing. If the customers' expectations are to be met, it means that management must have a good idea of what is required to promote the image and reputation of the enterprise or organization.

All workers are expected and required to give excellent customer service. Service quality is important to the organization, as it the quality of interaction between the customer and the individual rendering service that can make the difference in sustaining and driving new business. No customer, irrespective of colour, class, race, creed, ethnic origin, religious or political persuasion should be denied good service.

Front line workers are usually the recipients of hostility of customers who often accused them of poor communication. More often than not, the apparent poor service can be attributed to factors such as the poor personality of the individual employee, the lack of training the employee has received, poor recruitment and selection on the part of the employer, the limitations imposed upon the employee to use his / her initiative and or commonsense; particularly where the individual slavishly follows the instruction(s) given by the employer.

It is unfortunate that some employers are sometimes quick to lay the blame at the feet of their employees, when in fact the employer has failed to do what is required. Employers who expose their employees to training, can reasonably expect that the employees will deliver excellent service, and reduce the incidence of them receiving harsh criticisms and verbal abuse from the public when carrying out their assigned duties.

Customers can be justified in denouncing the delivery of poor customer services when their expectations are not met. It is understandable that the front line employee will become the target of the annoyed customer. It is quite likely that despite how courteous the employees may try to be, they might not be spared the battering of irate customers.

In a case like this, management must shoulder the responsibility for any such shortcoming. It is to be reinforced that management has a responsibility to keep operations running smoothly. If they are mindful of this, it is expected that they would be aware that should a customer have a bad service experience, the blame could ultimately fall on the establishment or organization. To negate this, management should seek to play a decisive role in ensuring that service delivery meets with the enterprise's standards.

Management has a responsibility to create a more customer friendly experience. It may require that an environment is provided where employees are empowered to solve problems. Further, in responding to the challenges of the time, it is important to maintain the loyalty and commitment of employees. What better way to do this, but ensuring that employees feel respected and valued by setting the tone for good customer service.

Whatever the circumstances, employees should be mindful of the part they ought to play in ensuring that the customer has a pleasant experience; and is satisfied with the service given. Providing prompt and reliable service, being courteous, polite, respectful and understanding are all required to be displayed in the delivery of excellent service.

CHAPTER 4   Guide To Retaining Employment

There are standards of behaviours and guiding principles that should be observed in a climate of economic recession or in a state of economic prosperity.

It is important for an employee to satisfy job expectations, if the individual is to position him / herself to have continuous employment. It starts with the individual believing that he / she can make a difference by displaying a positive work attitude, being prepared to go beyond the call of duty, showing interest and a commitment to the job, having the ability to multi -task (multi -skilled), availing oneself to training and specifically to courses that are job specific, and by developing a good work ethic that includes attendance, punctuality, dress, discipline, being organized and responsible.

Amongst the other standards that should be showcased are, having a good people and customer relations skills, such as being cooperative, prepared to listen, resourceful, making meaningful input, and being respectful and courteous.

It is important to show initiative, be innovative, be responsible, be accountable and trustworthy, show due regard for and follow processes, procedures and observe standards.

The showing respect for authority is extremely important.

To be health conscious and to observe safety and health standards are both critical to the personal welfare of the individual. These are determinants of your ability to do the work required.

Being productive and a team player weigh particularly high on the agenda of an employer when assessing the performance of an employee.

Be mindful that as an employee you are constantly being evaluated and observed. Don't disregard the fact that your retention can to a large degree depend on your attitude, commitment and performance.

Power vs. Authority

In any work environment, it is perceived that ultimate power and authority reside with the employer and / or management. This is rightly so, as these have the privilege to hire, fire, and make financial and management decisions that will determine the path the enterprise takes towards realizing its goals. It therefore stands to reason that with such vested powers in the employer and management, they are called upon to establish systems or operational procedures, control mechanisms and / or institutional regulatory frameworks for the purpose of ensuring that policies are implemented, and practices, procedures and processes are followed. This places an awesome responsibility on those who are so charged, as the onus is on them to account for their actions.

In exercising what is known as **'power'**, both the employer and management are using their ability to influence the actions and behaviour of subordinates. As the cliché goes, *'He who pays the piper calls the tune'*. This is practically demonstrated in the workplace where the employer / management can dictate what happens, how and when. Where employees may be seen as mere actors who wait to be directed, they nonetheless have the right to challenge the actions, policies and directions given by those at the top.

Employers will find themselves in a unique position from which they can influence the buy-in of employees. How this is done is another matter. There is strong support for the implementation of motivation strategies and for the incentivizing of workers, rather than resorting to coercion in whatever form. There should also be an appreciation that workers also have a semblance of power. The unionization of workers at the enterprise level and their ability to organize themselves so that a collective bargaining unit is established, means that they would have graduated into a position of strength. This allows them to influence intended actions, or to break the perceived ultimate power that employers and management assume unto themselves.

The exercise of authority by employers and managers falls into a different context to that of the wielding of power. It is a fact that embedded in authority is the given right to act. The authority to act is however governed by accepted guidelines, customs and practices, regulations and / or statutory regulations. This dismisses the notion or perception that the exercise of authority is founded in any form of dictatorial behaviour. Forms of dominant behaviour would therefore suggest an absence of discretion. In the absence of discretion, the wielding of power and authority becomes totally counterproductive.

Sociologist Max Weber in offering a perspective on authority identifies with its application in three forms. These were identified as rational legal authority, traditional authority and charismatic authority. He argued that rational legal authority is based on the observance of a set of rules, regulations or laws that are established by the state. Traditional authority is said to be based on traditions commonly called customs and practice. Charismatic authority is said to be based on the dictates of a leader, whom is without question, accepted as the chief decision maker.

Employers and managers who practice charismatic authority should guard themselves against working at odds, since their failure to act with discretion can only serve to undermine their own efforts. The wise counsel which ought to be followed is found in this quotation, *"Authority cannot be bought or sold, given or taken away. Authority is about who you are as a person, your character, and the influence you've built with people."*

In the final analysis it is important that a clear distinction between power and authority is established. Clarification of this is found in the definition that reads *"authority is the legal ability and authorization to exercise power for enforcement, while power is the actual wielding of the authority."* Further to this, there must be the understanding that power is the ability to affect change, and that it can exist with or without authority.

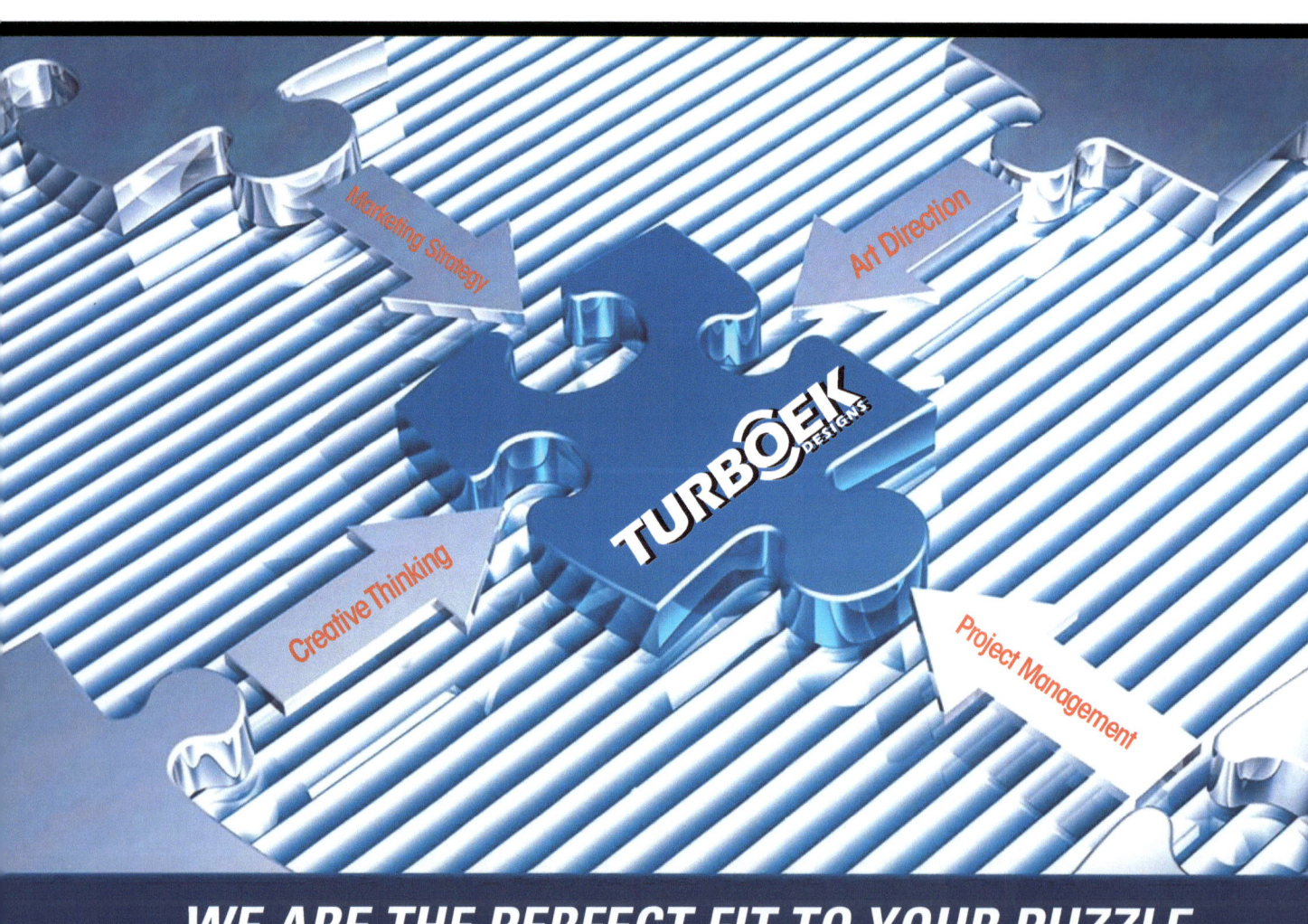

The Dictates of Leadership

Every new employee who enters into a new workplace, comes knowing not what to expect of the head of the organization or enterprise. The fear of what to expect can lead to some initial apprehension. As an employee grows in the job, this apprehension gives way to a level of comfort. Overtime an employee may find him / herself elevated into a supervisory role or even into a senior management position. Whereas at the start of a job it is good to know what is expected of your leader / manager, it is at the point of gaining promotion to a management position that the knowledge of what is expected of a leader becomes very important.

As a leader, every individual has to understand that he / she is expected to give guidance and, or, direction. A leader has to know his or her attributes and potential. These are best described as qualities and abilities. Being honest, responsible and confident, having the ability to motivate and inspire others, command respect and work well with others, qualifies a person to be a good leader. A leader should have standards, and set standards for others to follow. It is important not to compromise individual standards, so that these can be questioned.

Another skill which a leader should have is the ability to effectively deal with people. It is also an asset for a leader to possess good listening, reasoning and communication skills, problem solving skills and the ability to influence the behavior of others. The leader is expected to lead, and is therefore required to exercise authority, and to demonstrate that he / she is in control.

With respect to decision making, a leader should be equipped with good decision making skills. This has to be done with the understanding that the leader has to accept full responsibility for the decision made.

As a leader, one should involve and consult with others. This allows for the inclusion and participation of others in the decision making process.

Respect is another important attribute of a leader, who should respect the opinions of others. It is important that the leader is a good listener. The adoption of a democratic style of leadership should be adopted over that of a dictatorial approach.

A leader is entrusted with the responsibility of developing those who are subordinates. This means providing them with opportunities that would contribute to their development and growth within the organization. Effective leadership makes room for delegation of some responsibility. The leader must be aware that team building is an important part of leadership. Don't attempt to be a dictator, instead, include others in the making of decisions. A good leader shows vision.

Layoff & Retrenchment of Workers

The lay off or retrenchment of workers is an option that rests with the employer. It must be established that there is a fundamental difference between layoff or retrenchment and that of termination of employment. The difference primarily lies in the basis for the action and the procedure to be followed in the execution of the decision.

In the case of termination, this could be enforced as a result of the employee having breached the terms and conditions of employment, or where the employee's actions are inimical to the interest of the place of work. With the exception of termination or dismissal for reason of cause, in which instance the employee has committed an ungracious act such as that of stealing or lying, the employer is required to serve reasonable notice of pending termination.

The employer has an obligation to the payment of salary or wage, which is sometimes paid in lieu of notice. On termination, the employee is entitled to accrued holiday with pay regardless of the grounds of dismissal. As applicable in the jurisdiction of Barbados, on termination of an employee, the employer is required to provide that employee with a Termination or Lay off Certificate.

The lay off or, the retrenchment of workers is exercised by the employer after having determined that there is a need to reduce the operational expenditure of the business or company. In most instances the decision of the employer to lay off staff is based on the need to reduce the high pay roll expenditure. The slowdown in business also accounts for the laying off of employees. It is said that the layoff of staff bears no relation to the performance of the employee, nor is it a form of disciplinary action which is being imposed. In the instance where an employee is laid off due to a slowdown in business, the possibility exists that the individual could be re-engaged, should there be an improvement in the business finances within a specific time period.

Retrenchment is described as the forced layoff of workers by the employer. It is considered to be the termination of service of an employee by an employer for any reason other than that of punishment due to disciplinary action. The retrenchment of an employee has nothing to do with voluntary retirement, superannuation, non-renewal of contract, and / or the termination of employment on the grounds of continued ill-health.

Retrenchment usually results in a permanent separation from the organization. Conversely, the laying off of staff can be a temporary state, where an employee remains out of the job for a specified period of time.

The implementation of a retrenchment programme does not in all instances mean that there will be the loss of jobs. As the company or organization moves to cut or reduce any and all unnecessary spending, this might require reducing the size of the company, and this may result in closing offices or cutting back on the diversity of products or services that it offers. In such a restructuring process, staff members may be forced to revert to substantive job positions, which result in a reduction of pay and possibly benefits. Others may be required to accept reduction in salaries by accepting to take up lower positions or assignments.

At times, there are some warning signs that signal the possibility of layoffs or retrenchment. The slowdown of business is a prime indicator. The employer's implementation of a programme of reduced hours of work, or a short week employment, makes it quite evident. With respect to retrenchment, notice of the pending closure of an operation, amalgamation or merger, are usually clear indicators.

Where the decision is taken to retrench workers, the company or organization should pay all salaries (including unconsumed annual leave, notice pay, etc.) to the employees on their last day of work. The employee as entitled should receive severance payment, which is payable by the company. This payment is not taxable.

There are some best practices that ought to be followed in instituting a programme of layoffs or retrenchment. It is required that the employer acts responsibly and consults with the trade union as the accredited representative of the workers; especially if there is an existing bargaining unit. Further, it is expected that a notice period would be given to the workers of the intended layoffs and / or retrenchment.

The Principle of Last In & First Out

In an environment where layoffs are the order of the day, it is to be expected that workplaces will become a hotbed of tension, as employees wait in earnest to learn of their fate. In this instance, those who are temporary, casual or part-time employees are always the most vulnerable. In executing layoffs, the principle of last in and first out has been accepted as the guiding principle which should apply. This method is believed to be the fairest system in such circumstances.

Why is the system of last in first out followed? A case has been made that employers owe a greater measure of loyalty to longer-serving employees of the company or organization. Those employees tend to be more experienced, have a greater knowledge of institutional history and culture, and should therefore be more valuable.

A counter argument can be made that the last in and first out system might not be the fairest of all. It is quite possible that longer-serving employees can also be less disciplined, less productive and less valuable than the more recently hired employee. With this being the case, it cannot be ruled out that some employers would welcome the layoff exercise to rid themselves of those employees who are less disciplined and productive.

Where the employer acts in such a manner, it will be sure to raise a question about the application of fairness being applied. Is it right for employers to move to sever ties with an employee who does not promote the interest of the company or organization, and who more or less is a liability rather than an asset? On the other hand is it for employees to behave more responsibly, develop and display a better work attitude, show greater workplace discipline in being punctual and not frequently absent themselves from work?

Some would present the argument that instead of applying the principle of last in and first out when proceeding to retrench or make workers redundant, employers should opt to undertake a performance assessment of their employees. In this way, employers would have every justification in severing ties with those employees whose performance indicates that their continued employment is not merited.

There is merit in applying both of the positions when instituting a programme of retrenchment. However, it is important that when retrenching workers, employers are careful not to allow age or any other discriminatory measures to inform the decision as to who should be laid off.
Once the decision has been made to lay off employees, it is advisable that employers understand their obligation to pay the employees severance; and should be prepared to meet this requirement of the law, before embarking on a regime of retrenchment.

The application of the principle of last in and first out may be justified on the grounds that retrenching long-serving employees is very expensive, as severance payment is calculated according to length of service. Since retrenchment means the loss of a job and income to an employee, it should be an exercise that the employer undertakes, having given careful consideration before making such a painful decision.

Unfriendly Workplaces

Today's workplace can potentially be a hot bed of discord. It can be a place where a group of disgruntled workers can be found. It is also here that you can find individually dissatisfied employees, who hold the view that they are a target of their employer; be it at the top management or supervisory level. The adversarial relationship which exists is sometimes at the level of employee and employee. Whatever the factors are that lead to a break down in the workplace's relationship(s), the hard fact is that it all adds up to painting a picture of an unfriendly workplace.

Where such an unfriendly environment exists, it can lead to a hostile, volatile, stressful and unproductive environment. It is a mistake to think that this environment is conducive to getting the best out of people. The tension that exists can often lead to other ills that are detrimental to the workplace. No bigger problem could surface than that of chronic absenteeism, abuse of sick leave, unpunctuality and gross inefficiency.

This presents a night mare for any employer, who in turn faces a bigger challenge, if the actions of the employer is a contributing factor to the declining work attitudes that emerge. There is very often no quick fix to some of these problems, as it might require a complete review of management policies, systems and procedures. It might be that management is paying the price for its poor treatment of workers, exploitation of its employees, exercise of poor management and judgments, poor recruitment and selection policies, failing to communicate effectively with employees, and excluding employees from the decision making process.

It is easy to criticize employees about their work attitude, without having a knowledge of the conditions that gave rise to their behaviour. However, employees whose actions are callous and scandalous, must be severely reprimanded for such. Individual employees must be called to account for their actions, and if found wanting must accept the consequences. It is understandable that the difficulties experienced in the workplace can be depressing and demotivating. However, this does not give any individual or group of individuals the right to do as their please.

Grievance matters, disputes, personal issues and poor leadership stand out as four main factors contributing to an unfriendly workplace. Communication stands out as a single variable that has a bearing in these matters. If good communication was established in the workplace, it would certainly contribute to better relationships, less stress, deeper meaning, greater satisfaction, higher confidence levels and fewer misunderstandings and miscommunication.

General improvement in the relationship(s) that exists in the workplace, can be achieved through inspired leadership. Indecisiveness, incompetence and riding high on a big ego will do little to inspire confidence amongst subordinates, and to get people to work together in achieving the goals set.

Getting employees to buy in and focus on the goals of the enterprise, will help to move away from those things that might serve to otherwise detract from the mission set. There is also room for improving on the standards that the organization sets and for putting the requisite systems that will help to induce workers to conform, rather than to have it appear that they are being coerced.

It may be that employers do not pay close attention to the little things that count, which will lead to building better relationships at work. It is in both the interest of the employer and employee to make this happen, for it is the sure way to have a workplace environment that is warming and comfortable in which to work. This would certainly make for decent work.

CHAPTER 5 — Women's Rights

Protection of the Fundamental Rights & Freedoms of the Individual

The Constitution of Barbados provides protection for all citizens.
CHAPTER 111 of the Constitution of Barbados reads:

"Whereas every person in Barbados is entitled to the fundamental rights and freedoms of the individual, that is to say, the right, whatever his race, place of origin, political: opinions, colour, creed or sex, but subject to respect for the rights and freedoms of others and for the public interest, to each and all of the following, namely-

(a) life, liberty and security of the person;
(b) protection for the privacy of his home and other property
and from deprivation of property without compensation;
(c) the protection of the law; and
(d) freedom of conscience, of expression and of assembly and Association,

the following provisions of this Chapter shall have the effect for the purpose of affording protection to those rights and freedoms subject to such limitations of that protection as are contained in those provisions, being limitations designed to ensure that the enjoyment of the said rights and freedoms by any individual does not prejudice the rights and freedoms of others or the public interest."

The Labour Laws of Barbados provide protection for women. Two examples of such are cited with respect to Maternity Leave and Hazardous Work.

When can maternity leave be taken?
With due regard to the protection of the health of the mother and that of the child, maternity leave shall include a period of six weeks' compulsory leave after childbirth, unless otherwise agreed at the national level by the government and the representative organizations of employers and workers. [Convention No. 183, Article 4(4)]

*The Employments Rights Act and Maternity Act make provision for the protection for women during their pregnancy.

Hazardous Work
Hazardous work is defined as *"any type of employment or work which by its nature or the circumstances in which it is carried out is likely to jeopardize their health, safety or moral development."*
ILO Convention No. 182
(See Part V1..Section 73 SHAW ACT)

Right of Non Barbadian women to Work
Any woman who on 29th November 1966 is or has been married to a person who subsequently becomes a citizen of Barbados by registration under subsection (2) shall be entitled, upon making application, and, if she is a British protected person or an alien, upon taking the oath of allegiance, to be registered as a citizen of Barbados.

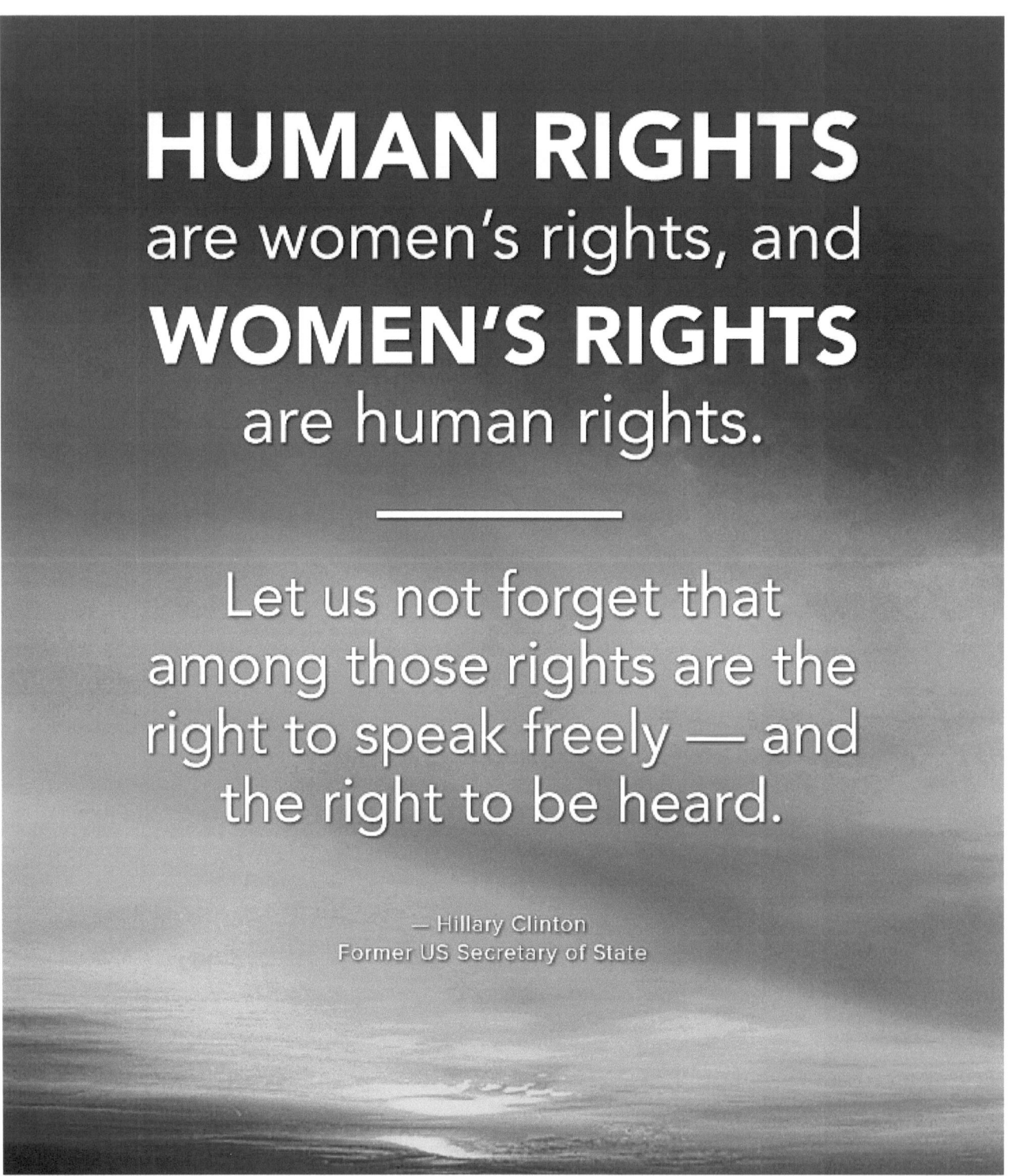

Sexual Harassment in the Workplace

Sexual harassment is identified as unwanted conduct of a sexual nature. Such conduct becomes harassment when there are continuous forms of unwelcomed sexual behaviour being inflicted upon an individual by another. Sexual harassment is considered to have taken place, where the recipient of such unwanted behaviour makes it clear that the persistence of the behaviour of the perpetrator is inappropriate. Sexual harassment is known to exist where the perpetrator is aware that his / her behavior is unacceptable but none the less persists with the same.

Sexual Harassment in the Workplace can be said to be present where any of the following are evident:

- Use of sexually suggestive words, comments, jokes, gestures or actions that annoy, alarm or abuse the other person;
- The initiation of uninvited physical contact with the other person;
- The initiation of unwelcomed sexual advances, or, the requests of sexual favours of the other person;
- The asking of intrusive questions that are of a sexual nature and which pertain to the other person's private life, or
- Where a person writes and transmits an offensive letter, electronic mail messages, facsimile messages, or transmits offensive posters or photographs, or makes offensive telephone calls to the other person.

Sexual Harassment may take the form of any of the following:
- Unwelcomed touching, grabbing, brushing or rubbing against, or other physical contact
- Comments that have sexual meanings
- Asking for sex or sexual favours
- Gazing and staring
- Displaying rude and offensive material, e.g. calendars, cartoons, pornographic material
- Sexual gestures and body movement
- Sexual jokes and comments
- Questions about your sex life
- Sex based insults
- Criminal offences such as obscene phone calls, indecent exposure and sexual assault.

The Grievamce Procedure

Grievances are concerns, problems or complaints that employees raise with their employer / management. Grievances are outcomes from misinterpretation or misapplication of the written company policy or a breach of the collective bargaining agreement and the common law legislation, as it pertains to labour management relations, or the established workplace customs and procedures.

Grievances may arise as a result of a number of issues. These may range from - poor communication, interpersonal conflicts, ignorance of rules and regulations by management, supervisors and employees, unclear lines of authority and or abuse of authority, environmental problems, health and safety issues, exposing employees to dangerous work, supersession, unfair treatment of employees and issues associated with pay increases.

A grievance procedure is seen as a means of internal dispute resolution by which an employee may have his or her grievances addressed.

To address grievances, employers typically implement a grievance procedure.

The grievance procedure may also be part of a collective bargaining agreement, in which there are procedures for filing and resolving grievances.

There are some principles that should be observed by both employer and employee in the handling of a grievance. These include fairness, justice, prompt settlement, due process, negotiations and bargaining.

At the outset, there should be an attempt to address workplace grievances informally, before resorting to the formal grievance procedure.

The aim of a grievance procedure is to encourage consistency, transparency and fairness in the handling of workplace problems or complaints. It should allow the employer to seek an informal resolution where appropriate, but allows for more formal proceedings should the circumstances demand.

(Michael Corcoran)
"It is not always who is right and who is wrong. But it is always what is right and what is wrong." Prof. M. S. Rao, Chief Consultant, MSR Leadership Consultants, India, **'Grievance Handling Procedure'**

The objectives of the grievance handling procedure are as follows:

1. To enable the employees to air their grievance
2. To clarify the nature of the grievance
3. To investigate the reasons for dissatisfaction
4. To obtain, where possible, a speedy resolution to the problem
5. To take appropriate actions and ensure that promises are kept
6. To inform the employees of their right to take the grievance to the next stage of the procedure, in the event of an unsuccessful resolution

The benefits of a Grievance Handling Procedure that accrue to both the employer and employees are as follows:

1. It encourages employees to raise concerns without fear of reprisal.
2. It provides a fair and speedy means of dealing with complaints.
3. It prevents minor disagreements developing into more serious disputes.
4. It serves as an outlet for employees' frustrations and discontents.
5. It saves an employer's time and money as solutions are found for workplace problems. It helps to build an organizational climate based on openness and trust. (Yourarticlelibrary.com)

The Grievance Handling Procedure requires that the complaint must be set out in writing and it should be specific to whom it applies. Provision must be made for the individual against whom a complaint has been made to be informed of the same and that individual should be given the opportunity to be heard before a decision is made on the matter. The party against whom the complaint has been lodged, has the right to be accompanied by a trade union representative, a lawyer or friend. The process requires that either party has the right to appeal the decision made.

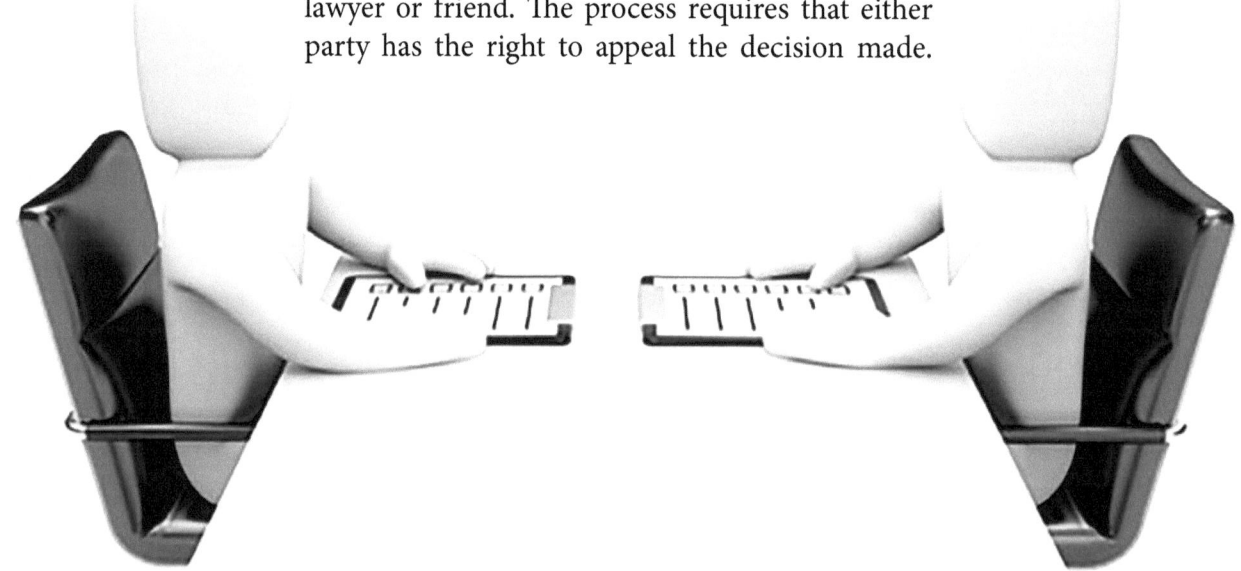

The Disciplinary Procedure

Employees entering into a new job have a responsibility to familiarize themselves with their contract of employment, terms and conditions of service, policies, practices and procedures within the organization. It is important to know of the disciplinary procedure, which is usually found in the Employee Hand Book.

The general principles which are set out in the Disciplinary Procedure include:

- Informal Resolution
- Investigation
- Notification of allegations: This is to be set out in writing and given the opportunity to be heard.
- Representation: The employee has the right to be accompanied by a representative to an formal meeting or disciplinary hearing.
- First Offence: The maximum disciplinary action of dismissal should not be imposed unless that offence is of a serious nature. For example Just cause, i.e. telling lies and / or stealing.
- Suspension: To place an employee on suspension does not necessary mean that the individual is culpable.
- Equality and Fairness
- Confidentiality
- Appeals against sanctions

Levels of Disciplinary Sanctions

The process includes a three phase approach.

- Written Warning: Employees are given a warning letter for any minor offence or misconduct.
- Final Written Warning: This warning is given after the employee commits a second offence
- Disciplinary Hearing / or Dismissal: This stage is reached once there are grounds that an act of misconduct has been committed during the existing warning period, which may warrant the dismissal of the employee.

Summary Dismissal

This applies in the instance where an act of gross misconduct has been committed. The dismissal takes immediate effect and there is no notice period or pay in lieu of notice given as a result of the dismissal.

Features of an effective Disciplinary Procedure

- Minimizing of the time which elapses between the act of misconduct and the intended instituting of discipline
- Advance warning to proceed any intention of disciplinary action
- Consistency in applying the disciplinary procedure
- Fairness and impartiality when dispensing discipline
- Private administering of discipline

The Workday

In today's world of industrial relations it is expected that the concept of a workday and the definition of what hours constitute a workday are unlikely to be contentious issues. These were considered fundamental issues as early as the 19th Century, when it was recognized that working excessive hours was posing a threat to the health and wellness of workers and to their families.

These matters were addressed in the first International Labour Organization (ILO) Convention in 1919. This Convention specifically looked at the hours of work in industry. At that time the Convention was designed to protect workers employed in some of the following areas - mining, quarrying, construction and manufacturing; whether be in the private or public sector. The Convention limited the hours of work in industrial undertakings to eight hours in a day and a maximum of forty-eight hours in a week.

Labour Ministers in their meeting in London in 1929 observed that the Convention stopped short of defining 'hours of work.' At the meeting, it was agreed that working hours would be defined as the time during which persons who are employed and are at the disposal of the employer. However, the definition did not include rest periods, during which time the persons employed are not at the disposal of the employer. This was later addressed in the ILO Convention No. 30 (1930). This Convention focused on the regulation of the hours of work in commerce and offices. It is to be noted that a definition for *'hours of work'* was included in this Convention.

It has been established that the universal standard of the hours of work in any one day amounts to eight hours. The move from a forty-eight to forty hour work week was as a result of the adoption of ***ILO Convention No. 47, 1935: 'Convention concerning the Reduction of Hours of Work to a Forty Hour Week.'*** It was said that the introduction of this Convention was a continuous effort which was aimed at reducing the hours of work in all forms of employment.

Today, there continues to be a tinkering with the hours of work in a day, and the work week. In professions such as nursing and policing, the option for a twelve hour shift has been pursued. The application of this will however run counter to **Article #4 of ILO Convention No. 30** which stipulates that *"The maximum hours of work in the week laid down in Article #3 may be so arranged that the hours of work in any day do not exceed ten hours."*

The extension to a forty-eight hour week is embodied in ***ILO Convention No. 57***, Hours of Work and Manning (Sea) Convention. The Convention which concerns itself with hours of work on board a ship and manning, provides for a forty-eight hour week, whereby overtime work is required for the purpose of carrying out ordinary, routine and sanitary duties.

Any redefining of the work time seems only likely, if this is done by the determination of law, administrative provisions, collective agreements, employment contracts or agreements between the parties to the same.

If there is any one issue which should be clarified under work time, it is that of daily period of rest, which is commonly known as *'the lunch break.'* This is not included in the working hours of the employee. Additionally, the time taken to travel or commute to work should not be included. It is only included, where travel from home to work directly involves work related activity. Such an activity, would be constituted as work time.

Thanks to the ILO, workers have benefitted tremendously from the international standards that have been established. These have promoted health and safety, the productivity of workers, and regulated daily and weekly hours of work, rest periods and annual holiday with pay.

In developing their understanding of the workday, workers should now be more conscious of the fact that overtime work is not part of their eight hour workday. It is not compulsory, nor can it be forced upon them. Other than that, they should be aware that based on the general trend, they are entitled to a period of rest after four hours of work in any day.

GLOSSARY of Terms & Concepts

A Team
A team is a group of people working together for a common goal. Success is measured. Each team member has a role and function.

A Group
A group may be a combination of people who have a common interest.

Attitude
It is the feeling or mental approach someone has towards something such as a person, object, or to their job. It is about the beliefs, assumptions and values we have, and we express these through our words and through our deeds.

Career
It is the pattern or sequence of work roles of an individual

Coaching
It is the art of facilitating the performance, learning and development of an individual.

Culture
These are values that are commonly held among a group of people.

Development
It is about bringing out all that is potentially contained within. Preparation of employees for advancement in the organization or for their personal growth.

Education
The providing of information and guidance in an organized manner to learners about all kinds of concepts and knowledge, both general and specific

Employer
Is the person for whom an individual performs or performed any service of whatever nature. Employer means the person having control of the payment of such wages.

Employee
Is one who is under a contract of service, even if the employment is casual, part-time or temporary. (Employees Handbook 1998: Barbados)

Ethics
These are standards of right or wrong, good or bad. Ethics are concerned with what one ought to do to fulfill one's moral duty. There are two aspects to ethics:- Being able to determine what is right or wrong, good or bad; and committing to doing what is right and good. Ethics is best described as the systematic study of standards of human conduct and moral judgments.

Evaluation
It is a process of objective assessment, job specific, meaningful and covers the period being reviewed. The performance evaluation process should always commence with a review of the job description. Consistent standards must apply in completing the evaluation exercise.

Globalization
This phenomenon is a process of interaction and integration among the people, companies and governments of different nations, a process driven by international trade and investment and aided by information technology. This process has effects on the environment, culture, political systems, economic development and prosperity, and on human physical well being in societies around the world.

Grievances
Grievances are concerns, problems or complaints that employees raise with their employer / management. Grievances are outcomes form misinterpretation or misapplication of the written company policy or a breach of the collective bargaining agreement and the common law legislation, as it pertains to labour management relations, or the established workplace customs and procedures.

Grievance Procedure
A grievance procedure is seen as a means of internal dispute resolution by which an employee may have his or her grievances addressed.

Human Resource Development
Human Resource Development is the management of human resources rather than the collective relations, and is therefore enterprise focus. It involves the individualization of the employment relationship.

Industrial Relations
Industrial Relations which is also referred to 'Employment Relations' or 'Labour Relations,' concerns itself with the state of the relationship between employer, trade unions and employees. Industrial Relations also concerns itself with Terms and Conditions of Employment, and grievance handling procedures that lead to conflict resolution.

Job
This refers to task or a piece of work

Just Cause
This represents grounds for immediate dismissal where the employee steals / cheats from, or lies to the employer. The courts will usually find that the employer had just cause to fire the employee.

In lesser cases like occasional tardiness or inattention, the employer should first warn the employee in writing, and give him / her chance to remedy any failings, before proceeding to serve a dismissal notices.

Knowledge
It is the information that is assimilated and retained by the learner and that can be recalled by him / her. It is about identification, recognition or recall.

Labour Laws
Labour Laws which are passed by Parliament, are meant to serve and protect the basic human rights of workers. These are: The right to freedom of speech and association, the right to non discriminatory treatment, the right to a fair trial (The right to due process in the workplace) and the right to peaceful assembly Labour laws are administrative rulings that address the relationship between and among employers and employees, and labour organizations.

Learning
It is a relatively permanent change in behaviour that occurs as a result of exposure to knowledge that informs practice.

Mentoring
This is the process of providing guidance, counseling and / or advice.

Motivation
This refers to a state of mind, desire, energy, or interest that translates into action.

Overtime Work
This is where any work is done beyond the normal working hours of an employee. Overtime may therefore apply where work is done over the 40 hour work week. It is not compulsory. The rate of pay after normal working hours is that of time and a half. Work done on public holiday / Saturday and Sunday that is an off day, the rate of double time pay applies.

Productivity
Productivity is concerned with how companies / organizations use resources (e.g. Labour, equipment, machinery, materials) needed to produce goods and services.
A nation's living standard is determined by the productivity of its economy, which is measured by the value of goods and services produced per unit of the nation's human and capital resources.

Profession
It is an occupation in which one possesses to be skilled. Any occupation by which an individually habitually earns his living.

Professionalism
Professionalism embodies the setting of high standards, excellent deportment and the exhibiting a of good and positive attitude. Professionalism dictates that the individual takes advantage of every opportunity, shares both knowledge and experiences, ask questions rather than to take things for granted, dedicates and commits oneself to assigned tasks, is innovative, takes initiative, inspires others, develops persuasive powers and is accountable.

Performance Gap
This refers to the difference between expected and actual performance.

Vocation
It is a trade, occupation or profession for which the individual has the required qualifications, skills or expertise.

Trade Union
Trade unions are organizations of workers that seek through collective bargaining with employers to protect and improve the real income of their members, provide job security, protect workers from against unfair dismissal and provide a range of other related services including support for people claiming compensation from injuries sustained on the job.

Types of Unions
Craft: This is for employees with a particular skill, e.g. electricians
Industry: This for employees in particular industry, e.g. coalminers
General: This is a broad union for wide range of employees usually unskilled or semi-skilled
White Collar: This is for clerical, professional or managerial staff, e.g. (Teachers)
Staff Association: This is for employees in a particular organisation,
e.g. Sugar Industry Staff Association

Training
It is the act of providing information and direction in a planned and structured manner to employees on how to accomplish specific tasks related to organizational needs and objectives. Training should lead to permanent behavioural change and measurable improvement in job performance.

Termination
This refers to the dismissal of an employee. In this case reasonable notice is to be given unless termination is for cause. Payment of salary or wage is sometimes paid in lieu of notice. On termination the employee is entitled to accrued holiday with pay regardless of the grounds of dismissal. The employer is to provide the employee with a Termination or Lay off Certificate.

Time Off
Minimum rest period is two days per week
Worker are not required to work on the day observed as the day of religious worship

Skill
It is the ability to perform a physical, mental or social task. Anything that requires practice is a skill.

Summary Dismissal
This applies in the instance where an act of gross misconduct has been committed. The dismissal takes immediate effect and there is no notice period or pay in lieu of notice given as a result of the dismissal.

Strategy
This refers to a systematic plan of action.

Strategic Plan
This is a document which sets out the priorities and goals of an organization for a particular time frame in keeping with the organization's mission. This plan should be in alignment with the organization's budget and organizational structure to ensure that these do not have to be changed and if changes are to be made, the plan should also detail—where the organization wants to go, and how the organization is going to get there and what resources are required.

Unfair Dismissal: Discrimination / Victimization
This is where an employee or prospective employee is less favorably treated because of race, sex, marital status, religion, sexual orientation or gender.

Wrongful Dismissal
If an employer does not have just cause to fire an employee, he or she is required to give reasonable notice, or compensation in lieu of reasonable notice.

www.ingramcontent.com/pod-product-compliance
Lightning Source LLC
Chambersburg PA
CBHW042014150426
43196CB00002B/37